# VIRGINIA POETRY 2025

1923
100 YEARS
THE POETRY SOCIETY · VIRGINIA
2023

# Collected Prize-Winning Poems
# of The Poetry Society of Virginia

First Edition 2025
Published by High Tide Publications, Inc. Deltaville, VA
www.HighTidePublications.com

Cover design by Terry Cox-Joseph

Printed in the United States of America

# Editors' Note:

The Poetry Society of Virginia is a dedicated nonprofit organization advancing poetry across our great state and beyond. It is the oldest poetry society in the Commonwealth of Virginia, founded in May, 1923. We are building a vibrant and inclusive poetic community, where poetry thrives as a bridge between individuals, communities, institutions, and cultures. Our mission is to cultivate the writing and enjoyment of poetry through a wide range of literary programs, events, and resources from regions across Virginia.

Each year, The Poetry Society of Virginia sponsors a series of contests which span a variety of categories. This is the anthology, featuring 52 first and 2nd Prize poems from 26 categories.

The Poetry Society of Virginia also sponsor an annual student contest from lower school to 12th grade, but those poems are not published here.

For most categories of the contest anyone may submit nationally or internationally after payment of a small fee. A few categories are reserved for members of the society or for Virginia students or residents.

All entries are through *Submittable.com* . Submissions open in late fall and close on midnight, January 19th, Edgar Allan Poe's birthday.

The top four entries are awarded per category and the 1st and 2nd place poems are published every year.

NO PREVIOUSLY PUBLISHED POEMS WILL BE CONSIDERED FOR THIS CONTEST.

Visit https://www.poetrysocietyofvirginia.org/ for opportunities for the 2026 contests. We welcome your submissions!

Dr. Kathleen P. Decker, Editor

# The Poetry Society of Virginia
# Contest Categories
# 1st and 2nd Prize Honorees
# 2025

## Category 1: Edgar Allan Poe Memorial

Any form. Any subject. No line limit.

1st Prize: "Ordinary Road" by Chapman Hood Frazier
2nd Prize: "River Glass" by Ann Chinnis

3rd Prize: "Entering the Summer Forest" by Michael Reynolds

**Judge:** John Hoppenthaler
**Sponsor:** Permanently endowed by the Poetry Society of Virginia

**1st**

## Ordinary Road

*(For A.P.C and A.D.C)*

### *Chapman Hood Frazier*


1


This red field's scar yields the best bright leaf west of Richmond
as farmers fuss about the weather, whether
it's too dry for planting or too wet,
recalling the summer of thirty-nine
when rain came like a missionary to the land.

Each ring around the harvest moon or unseen Southern Cross
below the horizon is a sign:
              St. Patrick's, the time to plant potatoes
              and when Jesus rose to seed tobacco.

Each harvest done by firelight is strung by women who speak
of pickling in the prickly heat as men
set curing fires for the all-night vigil
in the rack-stacked barn of cut oak and daub.
Wood split and stacked just outside the door

as children break from chores to watch the bull
stud just beyond the barn.
              Supper spread on a makeshift table till
              dark settles the landscape like crows on leafless limbs,

a time for gossip plied by a fiddle or banjo
and a hit or two of shine, the quiet whine
thick as woodsmoke across the vacant fields.

2

Or that's the myth anyway, reality always darkest
before dawn:  Moonshine run below the
graveyard's crackling fire. Each story wheezed
as either a secret or a curse. In
the sawmill's screech and moan, Luther's finger

sliced through bone.  Its stub wrapped in an oil rag to get the cutting
done.  Pain, the only throbbing prayer
                accounted for in a bottom line. Or
                old man Hopgood who shot his wife's escort

as they came back from Sunday school for sitting too close on
the buggy ride. One shot hit his daughter's
foot as she rode in the back carriage.
Only ten months in prison since jealousy
is a good excuse for murder in the

law's eyes if you own enough land.  Or a
baby born dead, buried
                in the front field by lantern light when the
                redbud blooms. Each child born later still plays with him

in the quiet moonlight of his bedroom. Grandma though
taken to the asylum in Petersburg
for nights of crying each time a baby came or died.

3

Seven babies in seven years and she, twenty years her
husband's junior, stoking each morning's cookstove
before the stroke of dawn to fix eggs and
gravy biscuits for the boys before field work.
Then threatened some nights or locked in for spitting

snuff on the bathroom floor.  Now, she silently rocks by the
window watching robins.
        The rain veined red clay bleeds into furrows beyond the barn
        as she weaves and then unweaves her yarn.

Down the road after supper while his wife and children watch
*Dialing for Dollars*, her third son, Alex, sets his books
straight, sips whiskey, then still in his work
boots and coveralls, shoots himself on the
bedroom floor. After his body is taken by

the ambulance, his younger brother buries what remains
near the pear tree, then wraps a shard of his skull
        in a handkerchief, a keepsake he'll
        place in his dresser drawer. Each fall when the sycamore limbs

shed bone-white in the moonlight, he'll sip brandy
and remember how each dream of a falling star
was the omen he'd come to believe in.

4

Now, cows push their noses through the barbed wire and turn
to watch me flicker cardinal-like between
cedar and sassafras before disappearing
along the highway's bend on my way home.
Drooling, they lumber towards the low ground's ooze

of mud and manure.  I pass a vacant porch. Its rocking chair
still, beside a churn of plastic flowers
        and smell the rain darkening the sky moving east from Lynchburg
        behind me as the light fades pale beyond cornstalks.

Driving the backroad home tonight, I see the blue glow
of a television from some darkened front room
and across the field see cows rising and
falling in the distance beyond fencerows
in the coming dark as the radio pulls

me home with another country song.
The road unspooling before me
Disappears into the cricket-laced night.

**2nd**

### River Glass
### *Ann Chinnis*

Sea Ray 360, Bayliner Bowrider,
Boston Whaler 480. I crave
those names – mathematical-hot,
like Tabasco glazing a fiberglass
eagle – as I wander the aisles
of the winter boat show & stroke

cold bows of V-hulls, pontoons.
But I love the heat
of an engine too – a fast, fast
4-stroke dual-outboard slicing
the Chesapeake Bay like a shark's
fin while I cinch my Ray Bans

tight to my head & hammer
the swells in a C-Hawk 250,
its Bimini top in a sexy shimmy.
I want to slide slick as a minnow
into the silky berth
of a 32-foot Chris Craft cabin,

but that's for when I get
both knees replaced, win Power Ball
& trade-in my Hurricane FunDeck,
which isn't much to look at,
but she's stable in waves –
easy to get into & out of
after a cocktail, which I never
do if I am the captain

& after I worked 24-hour
shifts in the ER – not wanting
to forget the sky's sapphire –
I used to nap on the river
in my second-hand Glastron –
– a 16-footrunabout my patient
sold me cheap when he broke
his ankle hopping into the cockpit –
where I loved to sleep
while seagulls screeched
& the salt water slapped
the hull, no people around.

Beyond all others, I loved my
first boat – a ten-foot fiberglass dingy,
me, Cleopatra with War and Peace
in one hand, a fishing rod in the other,
as my brother puttered me
around the wetlands. My father
bought the boat to get us out
on the river where we couldn't
shame the killing schemes he
concocted with his goose hunting
buddies, like painting an old aluminum
Skeeter to look like a cornfield
& baiting geese to a beached bass boat.

I felt sorry for my father,
that he was obsessed with honkers
& decoys & tricking geese
with a landlocked Skeeter. Those
are the finite things you see from a boat
in a corn field, but from a boat
on the water you see long necked geese
whiffling in for a landing & heart shaped
loggerhead turtles paddling
& U-Hauls bouncing on the blue
suspension bridge above you
& rain cracking the river's glass
as lightning splits the horizon
behind you & you count the seconds
until you yelp from the thunder,
thinking this time you are going to die.

But I love the feel of the hot
metal throttle when I lay it down
hard, the salt water stinging my eyes
while I duck behind a 4-inch windshield
& gun it home to the dock. Even now,
when I grab a wet mooring line
or hear fiberglass smack a creosote piling,
it feels like I am fatherless.

**Category 2: Sarah Lockwood Memorial**
Sonnet in rhyme and meter. Any subject.

1st Prize: "Interstate 81 Near Harrisonburg" by Steven Knepper
2nd Prize: "Drought Song" by Derek Kannemeyer

3rd Prize: "Sonnet on John 12:1-8" by Joel S. Neubauer
HM: "The Potting Shed" by Eric Forsbergh

**Judge:** Claudia Gary

**Sponsor:** Permanently endowed through Poetry Society of
Virginia in honor of Sarah Lockwood.

1st

## Interstate 81 Near Harrisonburg
### *Steven Knepper*

A crash congests the northbound lanes.
On Google Maps they're solid red,
clogged sewer pipes or clotted veins.
A moment's flow then brake light dread—
it's stop-and-go, but mostly stop.
In thick miasma of exhaust,
some fantasize a coffee shop.
Some fume. For others, hope is lost.

But do they see? Field-strafing in
A syncopated swoop and surge,
some thousand starlings slice a fin
through the sky sea, swirl back, emerge
above the smoking, stalled debris,
two wing-made wings to fly off free.

### Drought Song
***Derek Kannemeyer***

> *For once, then, something.*
> ~ Robert Frost

I'd found a whisper underneath a stone
I lifted from a creek bed in the woods.
It hadn't rained for weeks, yet something shone
in its scrubbed face, as if the crackled muds

where it lay plugged harbored a secret leak—
and secret waters, pooling in its veins,
breathed dews, to coat it with a sheen. A streak
of mica pocked the base with pinker grains.

A little hiss sang from the hole I'd left.
At first, all air, more like a punctured tire
than creek water, but then up from the cleft
low bubbles pursed their lips in a light choir.

I watched them pop. A mud seep licked the glint.
Cupped in my palm, my pebble dulled to flint.

**Category 3: Bess Gresham Memorial**
Any form. On friends and friendship.


1st Prize: "Crumbling Leaves" by Steven Knepper
2nd Prize: "Again Vietnam" by Eric Forsbergh

3rd Prize: "My First Friend" by Linda Partee
HM: "Marbles" by Mark K. Hammerschick



**Judge:** Stan Galloway
**Sponsor:** Permanently endowed through Poetry Society of
Virginia in honor of Bess Gresham

**1st**

## Crumbling Leaves
### *Steven Knepper*

> *I drink alone, for no friend is near.*
> —Li Po (Arthur Waley translation)

Young teachers at the crumbling boarding school,
we climb the creaking attics steps to sleuth
old Spivey's lunchroom tip. He says among
the props of movies filmed here for quick cash
in lean years of the school (one tragedy,
one comedy, but neither apt to stand
the test of time), among the podiums,
three-legged chairs, and globes with boundaries long
redrawn, there is, supposedly, a box
of Bibles in the KJV that once
sat racked in chapel pews. My friend's class wept
with mighty Gilgamesh for Enkidu,
and now they want to join the Exodus,
ninth graders he has stirred to love of lore
and tales of ancient times, old mysteries.
We find the Bibles packed up tidily
and then turn to the unboxed tumbling stacks
in the south dormer's sharp persistent light.
Some purge of downstairs shelves? A donor's gift?
Collection of a former English teacher?
A temporary stash turned permanent?
The topmost have no binding left to hold
loose leaves that crumble when we handle them—
heartache for two who spend their meager wage
on Faulkner, Kierkegaard, and Akhmatova,
who spend their nights in cheap beer arguments,
in the unending readers' seminar.

But deeper in the dormer's cache are some
degraded yet still sound enough to take
and read, including Chinese poetry
bound in torn cloth, the gilded title chipped,
red cover drained to brown. We read Li Po,
no burning bush but falling petals, wine,
and absent friends missed on a mountaintop.

A decade and a half have passed since then.
Dramatically unraining clouds boil in
the sky's scorched kettle overhead. The wind
lifts ghosts out of October's droughty dust.
The sycamores' shed leather chitters past
to catch in culverts, clutch on woven wire
and locust posts, tenacious till the spring.
I cup my hand to catch a dogwood leaf,
so dry it crumbles when I close my palm.
This leaf recalls those brittle dormer leaves,
Li Po, and you, my now long-absent friend,
the verses echoing across these years
still teaching how to live the emptiness.

**2nd**

## Again, Vietnam
### *Eric Forsbergh*

Hoang, were you that naked girl screaming
down the road toward us? It wasn't me that day,
weapon up, slogging past.  But I was close enough:
breathing jet fuel fumes, cinching bolts with safety wire
inside the white belly of a shark. Later, when

you were maybe twelve, did I glimpse you in the marketplace, behind
a table heaped with cabbage heads? From a C130, my friend Tuan
chain-smoked a Gatling gun: A bank turn released a ripping
sound, as he shredded both the shadows and the trees. Later yet,
as one of the boat people, you held your brother's body, drowned at sea.

Decades now, we've worked adjacent space. Shared
tea and coffee, slowly pouring out the details cup by cup.
You inhabit friendship like Buddha in a grotto.
A white lotus blossoms from your mouth. *How are you today?*
I reply, *I am your beggar Hoang. Grant us each a second life.*

## Category 4: Carleton Drewry Memorial

Any form. Subject: Farm life or working the earth.

1st Prize: "Trips to the Shade Gap Mill" by Steven Knepper
2nd Prize: "December at her Farm" by Eric Forsbergh

3rd Prize: "The Hungry Caterpiller" by Bill Ayres
HM: "The Ethics of Local Slaughter" by Lynne Schmidt

**Judge:** Fred Wilbur

**Sponsor:** Permanently endowed through Poetry Society of Virginia in honor of Carleton Drewry

**1st**

## Trips to the Shade Gap Mill
*Steven Knepper*

We're in the old red GMC. We talk
or tune the radio, ride silently.
I watch the passing fields or look at him,
my father wearing a DEKALB mesh cap,
wings on a soaring ear of ripened corn,
his long arm dipped in honey to the sleeve
line of his t-shirt where the muscle thins
again. His cheeks are stubbled like cut hay.
He needs a vial of cattle medicine,
some powdered formula for calves, a few
fence insulators, or some Levi Garrett.
"A dirty habit. Don't you start," he says.
It smells of rubber overboots and grain,
rat poison, iodine, and Swisher Sweets,
wood smoke in wintertime
and onion sets in spring,
the chop dust coating surfaces so thick
that devils swirl in bare bulb light whenever
you reach up on a shelf.
He lets me pick a Cow Tale, Mallo Cup,
or bag of M&Ms from cardboard bins
below the countertop. The checkout lady
smiles at me and asks about his crops.
Sometimes he lifts me on the feed scales, slides
the iron weights to balance out my growth.
One winter memory: I wander from
his side, approach the stove that groans and croaks
like some squat frog beside the mousetrap rack.
I slip the mitten, reach, and touch—and scream,
the finger flesh already blistering.
My father scoops me from behind like one
of twenty feed sacks that he bought that day
and whispers in my ear that it will pass.

**2nd**

**December at Her Farm**

*Eric Forsbergh*

*Quick! Open your shirt!*
my sister shouts out to my wife.
The newborn baby goat hangs
from her hands, limp from hypothermia.
The front door still flung open,
the herd jostles in the lot
as one mother nurses just the first of twins.
*She's rejected the second!*

It was always so with Nat, since we were kids.
In the Westerns at our local movie house,
if not the rider but the horse got shot, then
frozen, still with popcorn in her mouth,
she'd start with low moans of misery.
Mom and I would trade a glance as if to say,
-well, what could we say? That she's another breed?
After the saddest matinee of all, her heart
buried *Old Yeller* beneath her bed for months.

The motionless goat folds
against my wife's bared chest,
as she closes her shirt,
cold meconium smearing everything.
She prods an eyedropper warm with milk into
the newborn's mouth. We're guessing it might die
while time draws thin and barely breathes.
Then feebly, a tongue protrudes.

By Spring, bottle fed, hooves clattering through the house,
this agile animal would butt into the bathroom,
or anywhere my sister went for peace.
Natalie chose never to birth the human kind of kid.
Not every woman wants the struggle or the sum of it.
She opted instead to replace another,
a mother who could cope with only one.

## Category 5: Brodie Herndon Award

Any form. Subject: Heroism.

1st Prize: Oral Lake" by Chapman Hood Frazier
2nd Prize: "Reluctance" by Bill Ayres

3rd Prize: "The Sharpshooter" by Eric Forsbergh
HM: "An Unlikely Hero" by Laura J. Bobrow

**Judge:** Bill Glose

**Sponsor:** Permanently endowed through Poetry Society of
Virginia in honor of Brodie Herndon.

**1st**

## Oral Lake
### *Chapman Hood Frazier*

### *1*

Beyond the wooden boats
    harbored there, black waters
        opened to the two-tiered "Middle Pier"

where my mother would lift
    the slim arc of her body
        to dive from its second story

then swim back to shore
    where my grandmother waited in the shade
        watching me paddling across the Bull Pen.

### *2*

The concrete picnic table shaded by oak
    and hemlock was draped in gingham
        for the Fourth of July picnic.

While grandmother and my mother
    opened the basket of fried chicken,
        I floated there, tethered still

to the inner tube, alone in the Bull Pen, waiting
    till my mother waded in
        to lift me for supper and felt

on her wrist the strike of the snake that
    had coiled around my waist
        below the waterline.

Screaming, she held me suspended still
        above the dark water as though my life
                depended on it

as the water snake rose, then crossed the water
        towards the thick reeds and rockface
                of the other shore.

### 3

Years later, after she'd fallen
        on the bathroom floor
                the glass of her hip shattered,

I would lift her too with the ambulance medic and notice
        embroidered on his pocket,
                a red snake coiled around a staff

and remember the black waters, my tightening breath
        and the feeling of being safe, held
                suspended in air.

**2nd**

### Reluctance
*Bill Ayres*


Sure he wouldn't live to see things through,
When asked to serve—though he knew his reply was rude—
The first thing that the hero said was "No."

He watched others form in ranks to go
Then strode home and climbed back in bed,
Sure that he wouldn't live to see things through.

Each day the pictures in the paper show
Another body rotting in the field.
The first thing that the hero said was "No."

But after that, he wondered what to do.
And then he heard the way his best friend died.
Sure he won't live to see things through

He packs his bag and leaves to face the foe
No longer caring he might not survive.
Sure he wouldn't live to see things through,
The first thing that the hero said was "No."

## Category 6: Nancy Byrd Turner Memorial

Sonnet or other traditional form. Any subject.

1st Prize: "The Best Winter" by Aaliyah Anderson
2nd Prize: "Bound for Glory" by Mac Mestayer

3rd Prize: "Hellebore" by Chad Trevitte
HM: "Grief Pattern" by Courtney Cislo

**Judge:** Nate Perry

**Sponsor:** Permanently endowed through Poetry Society of Virginia in honor of Nancy Byrd Turner.

**1st**

## The Best Winter (Pantoum)
### *Aaliyah Anderson*


The etiquette, I recall, of death
      begins by chanting *stay away from me.*
So, I use my gloveless hands, working
      the best snow we can remember.

Bare oak whispers *stay away from me*
      as my heart thumps. This is no metaphor.
The best snow we can remember
      hasn't happened yet, but plummeting–

heart slow–there is no metaphor for
      the girl who makes herself late to
things which haven't happened. Not falling,
      my edges steal frost as I retreat inside.

The girl who makes herself (in extension) lewd
      greets no one. Norma's disappointed
in face. A triangle of flaking despair. The bye
      or beginning. There are more quarters than you

wish gravity to welcome. You startled
      as the boy answered, *Dead, I bet.*
Is this not the beginning? *Twenty five,* you
      insist, *isn't the worst.* The best, oh, we'd remember.

## 2nd

### Bound for Glory
*Mac Mestayer*

The train speeds by ugly broken backyards, scattered
bottles, bare dirt covered in weeds, cinder block walls
festooned in graffiti,
long-dead salesmen stare from faded billboards.

Flower pots, once joyful, reduced to shards.
The car's crowded, students stare at laptops, jamming
the aisle, new folks from the last stop.
Children chatter, an old couple plays cards.

Across sits a woman, pretty and slight,
holding a child, nine months, maybe ten.
He grabs for her phone with effort and strength but
when he moves his arm into sunlight

his hand glows, reveals the cherub from heaven.
Eastern Local, third car, coach class, seat seven.

## Category 7: Cenie H. Moon

A woman or women. Any form.

1st Prize: "For an Old Woman at Sixteen" by Derek Kannemeyer
2nd Prize: "Domestic" by Allen Weber

3rd Prize: "Value System" by Maggie Dillow

**Judge:** Joanne Durham
**Sponsor:** Permanently endowed through Poetry Society
of Virginia in honor of Cenie H. Moon

**1st**

## For an Old Woman at Sixteen
### *Derek Kannemeyer*

*Inside me I don't feel old. I feel the same as when I was sixteen.*

~ My mother, in her mid-eighties

Somewhere tonight she is a child again
with a cat mewling in her arms,
standing before a mirror in imaginary brocades.
Somewhere through an open window a shaft of moonlight
uncurtains the darkness enough to show
this shape of her filling the glass.
In three days it will be Christmas Eve,
and she has asked in her secret heart for this.
This gown the color of the sea.
These eyes the color of the sky.
How looking out over her turret she will see
break of day tinseling the lakes and the limbs and tops of trees;
and vistas beyond them of this country she is queen of;
and in a courtyard below, her people in dawn bustle,
some with their eyes raised
to the sky of her, where down she smiles.
Again tonight her heart lifts into an anthem from back before.
From back before I and a harder world rushed in
to fill them, her arms open to enfold it.

How much simpler
a life might be, if one could only want, and want forever—
not to have, or to become—only to feel, and feel forever, this frisk,
this shadow and cusp of having. Somewhere her cat
opens its pink mouth to mewl it down for her,
that age of ache, and longing;
down to the barefoot dark before this mirror;
down to where there is no other physics
but the heart's hoist of desire;
the slow wheel of the answering moon.

**2nd**

**Domestic**
*Allen Weber*

A summer dress drapes the ladderback chair. Her undone hair
sweeps the flour-dusted butcher block. Unbound, for now,
her grateful breasts rebound from every straight-arm thrust.
She's kneaded and covered mounds of dough; they're left to rise.

Hens cackle in the yard. Through the window she takes
a trembling aim, mouthing, Bang. Bang. Two town boys fall
behind tall grass at the edge of the road, alive
to bother her chickens with sticks and stones.

She punches down the yeasty balls (so they may rise again),
and reminds herself of slights and crisply ironed shirts—
her words so hot, the tabby flees her square of sun
that warms the beaten heartwood pine. The floor replies

as she shifts her burden, foot to calloused foot. She spies
her husband and sons, returning from a distant field.
The lengths of their strides measure her time to re-dress,
wring a rooster's neck, and wipe the mess from her hands.

## Category 8: Judah, Sarah, and Grace, and Tom Memorial

Encouraging reflection on inter-ethnic relations. Any form.

1st Prize: "Listening to Mama Creely" by Eric Forsbergh
2nd Prize: "Laundry Day" by Denise Wilcox

3rd Prize: "Learning New Recipes" by Jerry Hardesty
HM: "Virginia Minstrels" by Aaliyah Anderson

**Judge:** Dr. Patricia Hopkins

**Sponsor:** Permanently endowed through Poetry Society of Virginia in the memory of Judah, Sarah, and Grace, and Tom

## Listening to Mama Creely
### Eric Forsbergh

I questioned him,
    *But this is Vicksburg, 1968.*
    *It's nowadays.*
    *Why should it matter?*
My host nodded me off,
    *It matters to the Black proprietor*
    *and we're prohibited.*

We got ushered in
behind the nightclub's partition
labeled *Whites Only*
with a few other bleached-out people.
We ordered liquor and we listened.

But soon we drank a bitter honey flowing
from behind the sturdy screen.
Her roughed-up angel of a voice,
raw from pain and cigarettes,
rose uninhibited from a swelling in her throat
where justice must abide.

Bessie Smith and Mama Creely, kin.

The spirit grew and moved among her crowd
in the solemn and excited affirmations of the church.
Their hearts in torrent made me feel small.
Why had my mother taught me to refrain,
to refrain from crying with my sister
in her hour of despair?

I've seen James Brown,
sweat in bullets down his face,
his voice burning down the house.

How many more bullets and burnt churches
yet to prophesy from the microphone
of Mama Creely, Vicksburg, 1968?

**2nd**

**Laundry Day**
*Denise Wilcox*


She doesn't sort her laundry anymore.
Darks in one pile.
White folks in another.
Time taught her to disregard label instructions.
She finally figured out the rules
About water temperature.
They don't apply,
If you read them with your heart.

So, she tosses everything
She owns in the washer,
And hopes each person emerges
With the sweet smell of life.

## Category 9: Charlotte Wise

Any form. Any subject.

1st Prize: "Beautiful Briefly" by Elizabeth Black
2nd Prize: "Feeding Stray Cats in Ukraine" by Rebecca Leet

3rd Prize: "Last Supper" by Genevieve Watson
HM: "While the Dead Lie as Flecks of Paint" by Michael Hellman

**Judge:** David Anthony Sam

**Sponsor:** Permanently endowed through Poetry Society
of Virginia in honor of Charlotte Wise.

1st

## Beautiful Briefly
### *Elizabeth Black*

here the coast
here the sand
here the curled wave crashing
blowing brine-wind mist
into blackest night

ghost crabs scramble,
tiny pinchers threatening
us—the unaware lost
in thought

blindly printing footsteps
on still warm sand
beside the mythic water light

not stars
not moon
not swirling planets
but translucent peridot

bioluminescence
from the glittering dead

**2nd**

## Feeding Stray Cats In Ukraine
*Rebecca Leet*

As molecules of steel madness
concussed the air
and no next breath was sure

a vibration in his unbowed soul
prompted Sasha to step outside
and feed a posse of stray cats.

The offering –
from one displaced in the world
to others also beggared –
cost Sasha his right foot.

War presents, at times,
a tableau for tenderness –
often anonymous, usually unseen.

It always presents
a canvas for cruelty – unfathomable

yet undaunting
to the merciful who step outside
to succor the world.

**Category 10: Anne Spencer**

Any form. Subject: Overcoming adversity.

1st Prize: "When I Was a Mother I Was a Child" by Maggie Dillow
2nd Prize: "Validation" by Lindsay Li

3rd Prize: "Bedlam" by Ann Chinnis
HM: "A Fall in Autumn" by Mac Mestayer

**Judge:** Angela Carter

**Sponsor:** Permanently endowed through Poetry Society of Virginia in honor of Anne Spencer

# 1st

## When I Was a Mother I Was a Child
### *Maggie Dillow*

He used       his pinky fingers
      to slide long pieces
      of hair behind his ears because to use
      all his fingers to slip the strands
behind          he said
     was   *something a girl might do.*

     I've always been a girl doing things a girl might do
     like skirt bleached tines of blonde behind my ears

     using all my fingers beginning with the thumb—— [When you learn to play piano, you
learn each finger has a numbered name. You teach it to find Middle C, but when skirting hair it is
there to cup the ear barely touching and curved preparing for the pointer finger number 2 that
finds a D one note above. Near the ear the thumb is the first to find bleached tines and press them
gently behind 3 – 4 – 5 the fingers follow E – F – G middle ring pinky pulling in last and only to
lift itself above the others like playing tea party sipping from an invisible cup.]

He couldn't remember how to spell my name
     but didn't ask, just ended it with a "Y"
like it didn't matter that at 4 years old
     I cut with a stick each letter into the side
     of my mother's minivan.

He wasn't there of course    he was 14 years older, so 18
     then as I carved my name and in one year he would hold my first girl
     who is not mine
        although
             she is barely his. [He could barely remember how to spell her middle
name and when asked pointed to there being too many girls to remember each letter but her
middle name has only 4 different letters and my first name has only 5 different letters and the
piano has  7 letters
     A – B – C – D – E – F – G
     all he had to do was fucking ask.]

His 4 daughters have a mother his own age and she too had a hard time learning my
name remembering me best as *your father's slut* which was perhaps fitting but I was 17
and the word fit differently in my mouth then like something given instead of something
I could own and it wasn't anything I asked for

     so I thought about this when I wasn't having sex with him at 17 because I wasn't
     yet 18 as if the sun rose differently on my body and the way I understood my
     body in the world that day that made it different and better for him to touch when
     I woke up 18 instead.        I thought about this

when I woke up next to the youngest daughter at 4 years old her back to my back
and her body curled like a Middle C and her limbs sweaty from our closeness and
how she loved me with her arms around my neck when I woke up and how she
and her sisters asked me to play their favorite songs.

I loved them best I could but I've always been a girl doing
things a girl might do like trying to love girls best I could because that
is how you say sorry to girls with fathers afraid of what a girl might do.

When I woke up 9 years later
                at 26    I started running to the top of small peaks
            where no one came     where I could hear my name  spelled out right
                    into the sky
and at the bottom of a small peak he once jumped from a moving car because I wouldn't
say I love you because he couldn't spell my name because there were holes in walls and
broken hinges even when I used his name spelled right and because once he found a free
piano with an ornate piece of wood missing from above the side arm and he spent $250 to
have a new piece crafted by someone's hands who didn't know how much $250 really
was for us so I told him we could have bought anything else and his arms fell in and his
head hugged against his neck so I said *thank you* and the piano was perfect
and sat adjacent to the door
                he kicked in later
        where I was hiding from his hands
because to love him

meant forgetting my name until at the top
                    of small peaks I cut it spelled right
                        into the side of the sky.

# 1st

## val·i·da·tion
## *Lindsay Li*

**val·i·da·tion**
/ˌvaləˈdāSHən/

(n.) The way I dialed across an ocean / just to ask, *Am I okay? Am I porcelain, perfect / enough?* I was hung up on just for asking / for a dollop of vanilla extract, love, a china / cup of red ink. Genius / doesn't fall from the tree like Newton's apple, doesn't roll / through his brain toward destiny. Life is / louder than a song of Scantrons / passing through the hellish maw of the English department / grading machine: *name / date period*, envy forming a translucent shell around the solitude / of a barren classroom, desks wiped clean. I want / to hear your brain rattling as you nod, locked inside the lullaby of vetoes that shatters / my eardrums like the cracking coating of *tanghulu* / against the kitchen counter, fallen from the fridge. The way / I dialed across an ocean just to count / the number of times I heard *hotline / please hold* spiraling through the cord wrapped around my wrist, wrapped around my neck, *please / hold* on for more panic calls in the future, something / more than *yes no yes no yes* I'm waiting for / an operator who needs me to *hold on a second, miss* less than I need them / to fix their customer service department. Someone to listen / to my melt down at IKEA, at the table with the little "I," as in *I / need help, hello sir, hello, please tell me / where to go in the future*, as my future melts with the sugar / oozing from summer *tanghulu*, the *tanghulu* out of season, not winter- / chilly, after the rice paper and the skewer have melded / to the sour-sweet skin, as the snow that never falls in California continues / not falling, only unrequited appreciation puddling in my palms. I don't / shop for groceries without picturing you / nodding your head while we volley one-sided debates: whether we should / get cones for ice cream, if I will / ever make a decision without asking first. I should / stop telling and start showing. SYNONYMS: / *I want you to check me off / as a golden child, don't I / love you enough already, why would you ever think / what you've spared me would be enough?* USAGE / IN A SENTENCE: *Hello, how can I help?*

**Category 11: Handy Andy Award**
Limerick


1st Prize: "Ted's Haiku" by Richard Eric Pound
2nd Prize: "Hello Donald" by Mac Fryburg

3rd Prize: "Servility" by Mohamed Mohamed



**Judge:** Nathan Richardson
**Sponsor:** Ray Copson

## Ted's Haiku
### *Richard Eric Pound*

They demanded a haiku from Ted.
He submitted a limerick instead.
They demanded a change
Which was beyond his range,
And pronounced the entire contest dead!

### Hello Donald!
#### *Mac Fryburg*

The political congregation
Got sick and tired of inflation
So Biden got dumped
Instead we have Trump
The shit hits the fan in our nation

## Category 12: Strong Point of View

Instruction, debate or proverbial slant. Any form.

1st Prize: "My Roommate's New Gun" by Lynne Schmidt
2nd Prize: "Where Myrmechory Fits" by John Thornton Casey

3rd Prize: "Dillard" by Jim Garrett
HM: "How to Grieve Your Dying Friend" by Ann Chinnis

**Judge:** Kim Hazelwood-Haley
**Sponsor:** Anonymous PSV Member.

## My Roommate's New Gun
### *Lynne Schmidt*

My roommate is a responsible gun owner,
says the safe is always locked but leaves the bullets out.

Buys a Desert Eagle and says it's unloaded
*But put it in your hands,*
*feel how heavy it is.*

The first two weeks he has this new gun,
he brings it out daily.
He leaves it on the coffee table
as the dogs knock over coffee mugs.

On Friday he buys a new sight for it,
worries that the screw sticks out too far and looks silly.
When we watch TV he aims at the characters
and says "Boom" to the ones he doesn't like.

He smiles as he pulls the fake trigger.
I think about the times we fight,
the times he gets so angry his face turns purple
and spit flies out of his mouth like bullets
as he screams about how much he hates me.

On Saturday, he buys a new case for it,
tucks it into foam the way a father tucks his newborn into bed.
And as he sits with the box on his lap,
a gunman enters a grocery store
and murders ten.

**2nd**

## Where Myrmechory Fits
### *John Thornton Casey*

There comes a time when you listen to things – to all things big and small –
as on the first day of creation, anatomically-speaking,
some take to flying, others take to crawling.
Take your frantic ant as he or she scampers – first one way, then another – round and round
as if listening to some inner voice or some inner determiner – like a dream.

Not so the bee who has *real* purpose in life, is inner directed –
not by a flower feature, although its color or form may be dedicated to the invitation
to the bee.
Consider the large variety of vegetable-life the bee goes through to carry a flower's DNA,
in pollen sacks on its back, to the awaiting.

In the meantime, the queen bee is busy making supper for her children,
who will grow up and make honey for the ants, who have developed a craving for honey.
There comes a time when you listen to things and see a different point of view,
but no easy answers.

For example, I just learned about myrmecochory,
a process by which ants collect and hoard seeds underground for food
and then eject the uneaten leftovers from the nest so they'll be spread,
making the ants not frantic but ecosystem engineers of biodiversity.

**Category 13:** Alfred C. Gary

Iambic Pentameter. A historic event that occurred between 1925 and 1992.


1st Prize: "Vogue" by Adele Gardner

2nd Prize: "Kolyma Road, the Road of Bones" by Erin Newton Wells


3rd Prize: "Mussolini Gets the Trains to Run on Time" by Derek Kannemeyer


**Judge:** Lisa Russ Spaar

**Sponsor:** Claudia Gary

## Vogue
### *Adele Gardner*

The year that "Vogue" came out, Madonna showed
A homophobic world a way to love
And honor Harlem drag balls through the dance
That took the world by storm and lives today.
March 27, 1990, marked
The single's first release. The April vid,
With stunning choreography by House
Xtravaganza—Jose and Luis,
Whose talent hailed from Harlem "House Ball" fame—
Showcased the talents of gay dancers. Tours
Brought voguing to the world and lifted up
More LGBT beauty to the world.
Madonna showcased Luis and Jose;
Demanded rights for LGBTQ
And fought for treatment, research into AIDS,
Compassion crucial for equality—
Our icon for a reason.
                              My first "Vogue,"
a flash mob at my close friend's wedding, danced
with one night's preparation, lit the spark
for me to learn the anthem and to vogue
in celebration of my own late bloom,
a '50s coming out party, and pride
enough to share my truth with family, friends.

I'm glad to be alive and dancing still.
In dining room I watch Jose's Vogue vids
And practice spin and dip and catwalk, hand
Performance, floor show, duckwalk, and Vogue Fem.
I sing along while dancing through the "Vogue"
Forever linked in mind to my dear friend,
Whose marriage in Rhode Island stood among
the friendly state's new-legal same-sex bonds,
two husbands feted there with open arms.
So proud of him. Of us. Madonna, too:
Staunch friend and ally since her early days,
flamboyant art akin to drag, whose "Vogue"
she vamped like Antoinette at MTV's
1990 Video Music Awards
where "Vogue" won three from nominations nine.
This anthem brings me heart and soul today,
While I walk openly, first time in years,
Through business world and personal alike,
My outward look transformed to match the soul
Of man I've always truly been inside.
And as a Gen X '80s teen who loved
Madonna as a feminist as well,
I sing along in car, at home, at work
To celebrate the courage of us all.

**2nd**

## Kolyma Road, the *Road of Bones*
### *Erin Newton Wells*

Sometimes the cold is well beyond belief,
      the clothing scant, no gloves, a pallid hand

not like a human thing but numb and hard,
      the broken shoes, the feet unfeeling now

to make a body wonder if it floats
      in search of where the soul has gone, or if

it ever had a soul at all, this world
      of endless ice, salvation lost, their task

to scrape a road across a frozen land,
      a nightmare scar, with only simple tools

to reach and dig the mines, no food, or not
      enough, to fall and lie in snow, to seem

asleep as others lie nearby, no one
      to sign the cross or speak a word for them,

no plume of breath, these figures in a dream
      who lose the will to stand and cannot wake,

these winter lumps along a road that creeps
      from Magadan to what they call cold hell,

their bodies buried underneath, a grave
      so vast it holds one thousand promises

not kept, a thousand souls in search of why,
      a thousand names unnamed, a thousand griefs.

*(Built in the Russian Far East by Gulag labor during Stalin's Great Terror, 1932-53, where an estimated 127,000 workers died and were buried under the road.)*

**Category 14: Joe Pendleton Campbell Memorial**
Narrative poem about travel. Any form.


1st Prize: "Under the Shadow of Mt. Vesuvius" by Jane
Harkness.
2nd Prize: "On the Road to Nepal" by Diana Woodcock

3rd Prize: "Kayaking in the New River Gorge WV" by Eric
Forsbergh
HM: "Mesa Verde" by Jacqueline Davey


**Judge**: Catherine McCormack
**Sponsor**: Paula Savoy

**1st**

**Under the Shadow of Vesuvius**
*Jane Harkness*


Yes, I was warned about this place,
told to remain on well-worn paths
and walk about with naked wrists.

But what ills could plague a traveler
with Mary's face alight in endless household shrines?
Wandering away from the port,

where the coast buckles inward
as though a fanged dog
once gripped the land with its jaw

and gave the shoreline a good throaty shake,
I follow a Vespa cavalry through a cramped alley,
a dusty van bringing up the rear—

behind the wheel, two bored nuns
gaze at the crowds, plastic rosary
swinging from their rearview mirror.


Naples blooms around me, a concrete garden
of talismans—votive candles, faded icons,
Maradona's proud grin on a thousand flags.

Cherry-red horns and baby blue
charms with unblinking eyes
adorn the Spanish Quarter,

promising me protection from
the sort of bad luck that might
befall the city at any moment.

Under the shadow of snow-capped
Vesuvius, the ancient volcano like
a great ashen moon always rising,

I gather small blessings:
fingerprints slick with olive oil,
thimbles of espresso,

the puddled glow of gas lamps
lighting passages
where cathedrals block the sun.

**2nd**

**On The Road To Nepal**
*Diana Woodcock*


Once, I slept overnight
in a Chinese military camp,
our bus breaking down at dusk
somewhere between Lhasa
and the Nepal border.

Next morning, villagers rambled
around the temple grounds—
children with book satchels
bound for school.  Mist
rose off fields of barley.

Rooster crowing, dogs barking.
That feeling of wanting to stay,
the scene mesmerizingly serene.
Country air fresh.  But the bus, repaired,
sat idling, its driver signaling

it was time to go.  So
looking around long and hard
one last time, I vowed
someday I'd find my way back.
But we all know how these things go.

The air pristine, the land lush.
The memory precious—as if
I'd leapt the world's ties
and crept with Han-Shan
to sit among white clouds.

But the bus sat waiting.
On the road to Nepal, all along
the way deep in mountains,
green brushstrokes on the landscape.
I could have wandered ten years

in that border region, like Buson
in Japan's northern provinces,
training as a poet-painter
to meditate on the landscape
as on a mandala, fusing with it

at once conscious of every part of it.
Time becoming an eternal moment,
        everything in flux,
            linking and shifting.
I yearned to wander, to learn to decipher

the music of the weaving spider
as she plucks and tucks her silken threads
across the mountain paths.  I burned
to swirl above the barley fields
with swallows, to roller-coaster ride

with Bar-headed geese over the highest
Himalayan peaks.  To loft in meadows
shadowed around the edges by dense
forests of sacred junipers, no sign or sound
of carnage for miles around.

## Category 15: Dr. Lucile E. Thompson Memorial

Celebrating Women in Science and Technology. Any form.

1st Prize: "To Maria Mayer, Tu Youyou, Rosalind Franklin, Jane Goodall, Ada Lovelace, Rachel Carson And Others" by Lorraine Jeffery

2nd Prize: "Maggie" by Mark Hudson

3rd Prize: "Words" by Erin Newton Wells

HM: "Chrisine Darden-Soaring Beyond Boundaries" by Mike Lynch

**Judge:** Dr. Kathleen Decker

**Sponsor:** Dr. Kathleen P. Decker

**1st**

## To Maria Mayer, Tu Youyou, Rosalind Franklin, Jane Goodall, Ada Lovelace, Rachel Carson And Others

*Lorraine Jeffery*

In a world of *what ifs* and *maybies,*
you worked long grueling hours
thinking, considering, experimenting.

Caught in the nowhere tide
of scientific women
you splashed and floundered,
trying to add something
to the worlds of nuclear physics
anthropology, genetics,
marine life, math
tropical diseases.

Tied to history
like a boat to a dock
you hoped for a magic hat
while trying to birth a rabbit.

Sometimes you packed your dreams
like underwear, crawled into books
and test tubes.

Occasionally someone
threw you a life preserver
and for a time

you were able to
rest your strong strokes
and float
in the never-ending
ocean of ideas and
possibilities.

**2nd**

## Maggie
### *Mark Hudson*

A woman named Maggie Pocock,
is a space scientist who tends to shock.
Having a P.H.D from the University,
she strongly encourages diversity.

A scientist who deals with space,
she is a member of the black race.
She knew a lot of discrimination,
before building things for the space station.

In England, she hosts TV shows,
her dyslexia made it hard to know
if she would ever excel in science
but now she is one of the giants.

She has worked on a bunch of satellites,
and racism is something she fights.
Working on the James Webb telescope,
she gives women and the disabled hope.

Growing up, school was difficult,
her dyslexia haunted her till an adult.
But it turned out to be a blessing in disguise,
because the world would be in for a surprise.

Her favorite work she presents,
is building all of her instruments.
They measure infrared radiation,
she is a voice for a new generation.

She admits there is so much to learn,
that every generation takes a turn.
But she must've inspired countless souls,
passing the baton is one of her goals.

## Category 16: Honoring Fatherhood Award

Honoring fathers and/or their sacrifices. Any form. 48-line limit.

1st Prize: "Sonnet on Luke 1:57-80" by Joel Stephen Neubauer
2nd Prize: "The Stutter" by Maggie Dillow

3rd Prize: "Latching Onto Memories" by Diana Woodcock
HM: "Paterfamilias" by Erin Newton Wells

**Judge:** Kirk Judd

**Sponsor:** Bill and Michele O'Hearn in memory of Theodore Tomala, Jr.

**1st**

## Sonnet on Luke 1:57-80
*Joel Stephen Neubauer*


The baby, circumcised at eight days old
like all his fathers back to Genesis,
seemed ordinary, till his father told
him: "Son, God raised you up for more than this—
for more than age-old ordinariness.
Your life will be a prophecy writ wild
and where the world lies thick in wilderness
you'll lay the way of grace — *of God* —my child;
and this will be the way," his father smiled,
"you'll teach them all to trust the safety of
Emmanuel by taking what's reviled
and washing it refreshed for what is love."
  It's nothing ordinary, not by far,
    for souls to learn how wholly loved they are.

**2nd**

## The Stutter
### *Maggie Dillow*

started somewhere outside Bangor    erupted at Walmart
where we stopped to pick up a styrofoam cooler    Before Maine ran out of cities
Before we had moved to three different cities    Before we married each other somewhere in
the Northwoods before Wisconsin ran out of cities

The stutter sounded like he had never sounded to me: all hard cah's and soft sah's
Suddenly losing language like that made me love his language like that: all trying and
almost-can't   All thoughts erupting away from a surface of themselves *ah yes I choose you*
I thought as his tongue tied
him
The stutter started as his language started
then stopped at age 7  Started again   Stayed
dormant
until returning    24 years later for 24 hours    after a drive
in the dark through the night through the width of Vermont and a few hours sleep
at a New Hampshire truck stop—
And 15 years before falling in love
with my husband stuttering in a Walmart in Maine I was 15 and my mom made me
deliver food to a woman who presumably had no family with whom to eat Thanksgiving
dinner          which felt like fraud    We hadn't done anything like this before
So I stood    in the entrance    watched
my dad know to touch
the woman's
hands
She couldn't see      Maybe from cataracts    Placed each can inside her hand
cupping his around it announcing    *green beans    tomatoes    creamed corn*
pulling gently upwards to indicate where each can was placed in her cupboard
Announcing vegetables in a tone turned singular towards sincerity
Suddenly losing its Chicagoland ticks and quick quips short A's and surprise
wordsslurred          *nah I ain'tnever  nah hefullofshit*          Things my
Michigander mother considers a mumble
Surprises
in the middle of a sentence    How 2 words forget they can announce themselves separately
This is my language   too      Dad gave or else the city itself gave me
and I thought about then what my dad gave
to me and to the world
minus me
as I watched my mother watching him and it was maybe the first time I
understood how I wanted to love
another
and that meant knowing

their language so well
that to witness it felt
like a miracle

- 73 -

## Category 17: Ekphrastic Poetry Award

A work of art other than poetry. Any form. 48- line limit.


1st Prize: "Ending Credits" by Lindsay Li
2nd Prize: "Moon Games" by Kindra McDonald

3rd Prize: "Grande Odalisque" by Sage Cohen
HM: "An Apple Withers" by Elizabeth Spragins


**Judge:** Terry Cox-Joseph
**Sponsor:** Terry Cox-Joseph

# 1st

## ending credits for *Just a Girl*
## *Lindsay Li*

a lighter. a fake id. / a cheap bottle / of bartender's strawberry syrup / for a daiquiri / to save the world. or burn it / down, garnish it with lemon / on the rocks, gulp gasoline / and teenage euphoria on the drive home. in the prequel of self-destruction, you tried / to curry favor with a potential boss / post-interview, over chicken katsu at the run-down shack in which you've / loved, first-time handholding and a pathetic plea to die / together, *till humanity tears me apart.* someway down the series, you'll find yourself in / a summer course on anthropology / wondering how we evolved to rise and fall, burning out triumphantly / with a professor who offers you a *wild ride* / for an a+. neither will truly fill / the voids in you—but they're the suitors / you'll quote in captions down the road / & you're *just a girl.* in the reverie of / sinful dreams, that girl wishes for lover's reprieve. we call it ecstasy of living. you meet another girl who / brings you hair ties at a party, knows how to / pull it back while you cough shirley temples of blood into the sink. *i did this before you*, she says to her protégé. the audience of deluded ancestors wants a fight and the tickets won't sell without action. in her hair, there's a glass swan that refuses to use its wings. in the night air, a bruise / dilates on your right arm like a pupil & you choke / on the tail of *promise you won't let go* when / you say it. when she leaves you / in the parking lot, god drops a shooting star & you catch / a taste of its bliss / in your palm. the world isn't full / of strawberry air, only metastasizing / into the unnamed wish of syrupy joy.

**Link To "Just a Girl" on YouTube:**

https://youtu.be/
PHzOOQfhPFg?si=EnowpECr2N3qa8q5

**2nd**

## Moon Games
### *Kindra McDonald*

"Moon Games" By Jenny L. McNutt

What you cannot know
is why we dance with the moon

huge pearl on the clouds—
guide us upwards

the ground is our trampoline
we cartwheel forward

bound higher, leap sure-footed
in the unquiet night.

Moon, sing us joy, sing us color
blue back spirals of ears

swish of tails, our fur is fire
our eyes coal, and deep in that place—

that soft pink of our ears—
we hear what you never will.

Our play is rite, ritual, carnal
and pure, we are so much more

than creature, trickster, pet. We are
mirror to every barrel aimed, so much more

than gravity's hold on us. Green, we want you
green and trembling, snuggle, struggle, strangle

luna consort, our will to live is vivid
twitching like a leg in a snapped trap.

## Category 18: Joanne Scott Kennedy Memorial

New Voices. Only open to poets who have never won a 1st, 2nd or 3rd prize in any PSV contest. Any subject. 48-line limit.

1st Prize: "Someday I'll I Love Summer Again" by Adelaide Sendlenski
2nd Prize: "Triptych for a Hypothetical Deceased Evil Mother" by Lindsay Li

3rd Prize: "Sailing" by Fran Scott
HM: "Dear Dad, I Wrote this Poem for Mom" by Cammie Fuller

**Judge:** Kristin Zimet
**Sponsor:** Dr. Sofia M. Starnes

**1st**

## Someday I'll I Love Summer Again
### *Adelaide Sendlenski*

Summer boiled in its brittle shell. Dad left no forwarding address. Tire marks streaked our front lawn yellow until the gods finally cried. I couldn't peel the meat from the lobster; I couldn't crack its armor. Mum said lobsters can't feel pain. As she cooked, I watched papaya-seed eyes pop in the boiling water. A lobster's pain was the absolute value of its need to escape. Maybe dad's was, too. A man in a blue shirt hammered a *for sale* sign into the mouth of wilting hydrangeas. Mum milked tears from her drywater eyes. The hydrangeas were once her pride and joy. I rode my bike everywhere and nowhere. I pedalled as hard as I could, until the trees raced backwards. I pedalled until the sky stood still and I gasped for air. Plump cherries in plastic sleeves filled our fridge. I loved cherries, the sting of their sweetness. They dyed my teeth purple, left the rims of my nails sweet. But I couldn't bring myself to eat any. I couldn't stand the spat-out seeds and the bellyache. I wished for winter, for numb fingers and brittle nights of rimy solitude. I wished for everything that was not, until we packed a rubbish bag full of *not anymore*: his rough brown flips flops, faded t-shirts still damp with memories. Mum and I drove to the Salvation Army in watery silence. After, I lay in his empty closet and clung to the *i love you* he muttered as his car rolled away. He rolled away like a marble down a drain. It was hopeless, so I swam in the ocean. I sold the salt of my sadness to the Atlantic. Floating on my back, I prayed for the ocean to swallow me whole. That night, I dreamt I was a baby cradled in a lobster trap. I woke sobbing.

# 2nd

# Triptych for a Hypothetical Deceased Evil Mother
*Lindsay Li*

妈 dies on a Thursday evening. She is already exploding into ashes, first from her cigarette-sooted hand. Soon others will follow: the hair she stopped dyeing at 50, the heart that jumped one time too many, the thawing smile on her face without saying goodbye. *At last I'm done with you.* Tomorrow morning I'll cinch a funeral dress until I stiffen into her halfhearted marionette, our shared genesis irrevocably stringing us together. I could fly eight-hundred eighty eight miles from my hometown and yet the familiarity returns to her, always 百善孝为先, daughter bowing until her heart pierces the floorboards. 妈 called her children "issue" like faux royalty until they were no longer her problem. When I draw the curtains, the moon slowly blinks back at me in a breathless house.

We, two women, pondered around a desk as 妈 stained my nails pomegranate red for the first time. Years ago, I still couldn't keep my nails intact, turning them into papier-mâché every month, clamping down hard on skin. She thought red was lovely power. I only knew how to draw my own blood, through gaping craters once the baby teeth spilled out. 妈 taught me how to spit discarded fangs into napkins, how to crack a candied sunflower shell without crushing the origin at the center. Muscle memory would prove a curse, my taste buds cramping after Chinatown merchants offered me handfuls of toasted chestnuts. I despised the taste and then the sound. My fingernails dart to my lips, honey-glazed with polish. There's no hesitation before I bite down.

妈妈, stay with me. Play the game where you are the hen and I, the frail chick clinging to you like I still love you. Someday, I will take your book of fables and sit cross-legged on the altar, watch the golden ornaments I was named after shatter without morals to lead them. Tonight I will dance for the first time since I quit, your residual sobriety as my witness. Join me, 妈妈. 好事成双: good things come in pairs, like silver shoes and the sable rabbits you brought home. It takes two to tango and I could never escape the frigidity of your hands, cupping cigarette flames at the kitchen table long after the meal is over. In tonight's dreams, I see those rabbits, bounding away in the dead of night, the cage door swinging open in my hand. You join me on the grass, reborn like morning dew.

妈 — mother
妈妈 — mommy, affectionate term for mother
百善孝为先 — "of all virtues, filial piety comes first"
好事成双 — "good things come in pairs"

## Category 19: Elizabeth J. Urquhart Memorial

A sense of place. Places-man-made, natural, personal, or historical inform poetry with the power to evoke the past and transcend the present. 48-line limit.

1st Prize: "Oświęcim" by Mark Hammerschick
2nd Prize: "Where You Wrote" by Jacqueline Davey

3rd Prize: "Kailua-Kona Island" by Diana Woodcock
HM: "An Old Hotel in Norwich" by Adele Gardner

**Judge:** Patsy Asuncion
**Sponsor:** Mary M. DeLara & Guy Terrell

**1st**

## Oświęcim
### *Mark Hammerschick*

I am a whorled spectre
sluicing salacious thighs

sliced diced fingers
bleeding rice worm

whistles in dead crystal night
miles to go before the trains

where does loam go
burning singed ice

cauterized cries
as the gas descends

bricks melt ooze bruise
eyes disguised as lice

decadent patterns
of flesh chained to cotton candy spikes

retching lighted yellow nerot
the sound a femur makes when it breaks

it's like that
speckled recalcitrance

scattered glitter flirting
with your iris

rings hair shoes fingers
jelly jammed joolishness

gloaming roaming wide
light speed infinite

ovens growl howl bowels
Arbeit Macht Frei

## Where You Wrote

**_Jacqueline Davey_**

_~Dylan Thomas in Wales_

At the edge of town
I cross a cobbled bridge
over the mossy creek
where water threads
between stones
and carries your voice.

Along the long quay
where gulls linger
as fishermen cast long rods
into the green sea.

Keeping to the gravel path
whose curve reveals a broad view
across the lapping water
before turning up into trees.

At the top of the hill
the little boathouse rests quietly
green with an off-centered door.

Inside, your dusty tweed jacket is draped
over the chair pushed back from the desk
scattered with papers you left as if gone
for a short stroll.

I peer out the windows
at your view of the bay
and white dotted slopes of distant farmland.

Here the ritual of sea, boats,
and herons called your name
and white tips of perennial waves
spoke of youth and aging and, always,
of coming change.

All that pulled you back time and again
to this place that harbored the universe.

**Category 20. Jeffrey Hewitt Memorial**
Social commentary. Any form.


1st Prize: "Panic Attacks at Dawn" by S. Preston Duncan"
2nd Prize: "Ballad for Viriginia Beach" by Adelaide Sendlenski

3rd Prize: "Another Mass Shooting" by Lynne Schmidt
HM: "Working on Second Sight" by James Huneycutt



**Judge**: Joanna Lee
**Sponsor**: Friends of Jeff Hewitt, (Jill M. Winkowski and others)

**1st**

## Panic Attacks at Dawn

### *S. Preston Duncan*

All of Europe is grieving.
An artificial sun rises in the West
and they see it is a nation of torches
wearing the mask of dawn.

In Italy a woman weeps into her olive trees.
Her face is a volcano that flows with oil.
By the stove she says *once this was sacred*
*and we anointed our warriors and priests*
*with the year's fallen fruit.*
*Now it is the labor of machines*
*and I have not even a bottle left to give.*
*Now you will return to the sun empty-handed.*

In Paris the cafés are still.
Only the light remembers music.

It rains more,
rain digs beds into the mountains
for clouds of mosquitoes
that know the shape of America,
that fly like a flag of war over the continent.
Every land is a country invaded;
their colors run into a sea
that drowns the anthem of the season.
Drowsy waves with their drowsy melodies
quieting upon the shore.

Farmers with baskets of stone march hungrily into the morning.
The towns are full of dust merchants
offering their throats to the sky

which is a blue bomb waiting to form the names
of the fallen,
for the new sun to press its red button
into the wound of the world.

## 2nd
### Ballad for Viriginia Beach
### *Adelaide Sendlenski*

we braid the snakes of your sunset.
we ripple with the pool's pleated veins.
we watch shards cast on open water.

we unfurl the fins of a striped bass.
our fingers are caked with childhood, worms
& mud pies, & we comb the highway—hands

like lanterns, phosphorescent beacons in the backseat.

mac miller shakes the car at volume 40:
we plant waves of sarcasm in the mind
of the man with the **VOTE NO ONE 2024** sticker

plastered on his honda civic. we plunge

our youth into your sand bucket.
we grip the spade in spoonfuls, our hands
so willing. we search the surf for sand-crabs

& their illusory feelers. my father's hands

cup a handful for my collection, after the fridge bloomed
with fourth of july costco deals—2-for-1
barbecuing packages, a 20-pack of Haagen-Dazs.

we watch the house melt into silt and fried tides—
until the **SOLD!** sign droops the hydrangeas, deflates
the cinnamon grass striped with tire-marks, grazes
the movers defiling 10-year-old drawings with yellowing
sticky tape, lost a tupperware box of dolls we once blessed

with haphazard hair, paper money spiraling in pockets
of the driveway's wind—*in virginia beach*, my grandmother

always said, *certain houses reek of divorce*. previous owners
cultivate them, no doubt passing on a shoal of self-doubt—
virginia beach, our house stands by the bay and laments

the tide's shortcomings: the pine-needled pool, the belligerent

frogs musking in the dock greens. tattered
wood crusting with nacreous oysters. happy fourth
to the rows of colonial american motels.

to the bay's cool glass american noodles, to the boiling
american crawfish and clams nestled in american
bacon. to the american strip malls in their hulking

american glory. to the tinny american voice
of the drive-thru speaker, to our american luminosity
in our sweltering american heat, to the family

standing on 32nd Street, guzzling the american sky.

**Category 21: Alexandra "Zan" Delaine Hailey Memorial**

Inspired by an artist or creator across disciplines. Any form. 48-line limit.


1st Prize: "Goldfinch on Thistle" by Chapman Hood Frazier
2nd Prize: "Feather" by Erin Newton Wells

3rd Prize: "O'Keefe Country" by Roseanne Walters
HM: "The Forewing of a Comma" by Sarah Kohrs



**Judge:** Dr. Luisa A. Igloria
**Sponsor:** The Hailey Family

**1st**

# Goldfinch on Thistle
## *Chapman Hood Frazier*

What begins as dun-colored
　　　goldens in this alchemy of spring.  It settles on a purple thistle's bloom
　　　　　　flickering black wings
　　　　　　　　in this morning sun.

Each prophesy begins in what's noticed, felt into.  Each season's remembrance
　　　in the signature of wind, a sacred sign
　　　　　　　　appearing in the pine pollen that settles on the windshield
　　　　　　　　　　or heard in the repeating cheep of Goldfinch.

Picasso said they ought to put out the eyes of painters as they do Goldfinches
　　　in order that they might better sing. Perhaps, creativity is sacrifice
　　　　　　　　in the pursuit of the ineffable.

A goldfinch knows the meaning of sacrifice in the plucking of thistle seeds
　　　or like the Celtic seer Brigid can tell if someone sick
　　　　　　　　may live or die.

An Iroquois legend tells how a goldfinch brings sunlight to yellow the fox's grief.
　　　And for the ancient Egyptians
　　　　　　　　it brought the message of afterlife.

Under the chapel of St. Oswald's church in the Black Forest, I saw a scattering
　　　of bones, a sign that each season weathers us all white in time
　　　　　　　　but like the bird held in the Christ Child's hand

　　　in Raphael's *Madonna of the Goldfinch,* perhaps this too is a season's
　　　　　　　　secret held in this brief moment
　　　　　　　　　　still golden in our hands.

Wood Engraving by Christopher Register
Farmville, VA

*This piece is inspired by a wood engraving, The Goldfinch by Virginia artist Christopher Register; however, it references other artistic depictions as well. This is a copy of the actual wood engraving.*

# 2nd

## Feather

### *Erin Newton Wells*

*(In gratitude for Emily Dickinson, who opened up
a new way of poetry for me when I was a child.)*

Just when needed, found, quite young,
in search of something new
beyond the everlasting trap of rhyme
memorized in school.

A way, at last, to let the sound run free,
mingle and converse,
not in rigid march step, this,
or drumbeat to comply.

A conversation flowed,
like waves upon familiar shore,
but had the strength of ocean at its back.
I wanted this.

Such ordinary things she saw,
I saw them, too.
She gave me leave to speak of them
as simply as a feather falls.

## Category 22: Hardy Haiku
Three to four related haiku (i.e. a series)


1st Prize: "Backyard Birds" by Elizabeth Black
2nd Prize: "Shipped Oars" by Derek Kannemeyer

3rd Prize: "Haiku" by David Partie
HM: "Haiku" by Catherine Puma



**Judge:** Randy Brooks
**Sponsor:** Anonymous long-term PSV member

**1st**

### Backyard Birds
*Elizabeth Black*


the hybrid rose
goes rogue...
refuge for a house wren

moonlight...
the mockingbird
chiaroscuro

savoring the taste
of fresh honeycomb
vireo song

summer picnic...
sparrows not waiting
to be invited

**2nd**

### Shipped Oars
### *Derek Kannemeyer*


my shipped oars
light's dribble
of bird song

my uncupped hands
fish scribble
inks the shallows

this wind in the willows
tattered tree dapple
adjusts its parasol

this wheeze of breath
is mine then
still

## Category 23: Climate Change

The gravity of the climate change crisis and the vulnerable state of our environment.

1st Prize: "Premonition" by Laura J. Bobrow
2nd Prize: "In Receipt of Fire" by Maggie Dillow

3rd Prize: "Los Angeles" by Ashley Mo

**Judge:** Dr. Laura Bylenok
**Sponsor:** Anonymous PSV Member

## Premonition
### *Laura J. Bobrow*

The prescient trees have come awake.
They turn their leaves up to the sky.
There is a storm about to break.

In fear the speckled rattlesnake
seeks shelter where the earth is dry.
The prescient trees have come awake.

I still have old amends to make.
The climate's changed, and we may die
within the storm about to break.

My limbs are weak. My innards shake.
The floods and earthquakes multiply.
The prescient trees have come awake.

I tremble. Dark mists overtake
our troubled world. They signify
the final storm is soon to break.

If only we might yet forsake
those ominous clouds. But though we try,
the prescient trees have come awake.
There is a storm about to break.

**2nd**

## In Receipt of Fire
*Maggie Dillow*


The maps in Northern
Minnesota don't fragment
with gas station Christmas trees,
no white empty lights
tugging empty tanks
from town to town to sleep.
       Rather signs to remind you to find your fuel and fill your
       car your belly your heart before the road runs out of towns. Here
there is hardly room between
the mandible and the dirt
it came from.  Straight through
and simple as anything; a line, fixed and sure:
the hare's rambling ligature
woven into the steady indent
of grey wolf struts, toe-to-talon delimitation
mushroomed out to the edges
of interrupted snow.
       Moving with certainty, or else shrieking wildly in the dark,
       it is hard to tell, to know, who or what is as petulant as a person
with their mind making up
what the world means and has
to offer. Back home in Northern
Illinois there are no wolves, rather the lilt of lightning bugs
murmuring on the hem
of Kentucky bluegrass stalks,
frothy seeds planted in even square chunks
before school starts up again.

**Dillow,** In Receipt of Fire, cont'd.

And it is quiet as we know
no matter how far ahead
of surviving we have come—
        When the heat arrives here, for us
        for our children running to the bus,
        we will watch in receipt of fire
        a swollen throat on its knees
        head thrown back,
        an offering.

## Category 24: Family Relationships
Family. Any Form. 45-line limit.


1st Prize: "The Last Drawer" by Minnie Wu
2nd Prize: "Interim" by Lindsay Li

3rd Prize: "Ode to resistance, After" by Adelaide Sendlenski
HM: "Elergy After the Pandapocalpyse" by Julianne Pan



**Judge:** Henry Hart
**Sponsor:** Diana Kincannon

## The Last Drawer
### *Minnie Wu*

Over tomato and egg soup, Mom said
    she still remembered the afternoons

she walked to the post office, miles
    north of her dorm, to mail

each letter she mailed to Dad. It was
    1997, *Xi'an*—five pages

per envelope. I never imagined
    Mom as chatty, love-

struck—instead, our house was
    silent. Housework. Homework.

Expenses. Debates over which grocery store
    had jumbo carrots on sale

even though we didn't even like them.
    *Eat, Millie, it's good for Vitamin A.*

While forcing myself to slurp
    each spoon of carrot soup, I asked

what she wrote into those
    withered-yellow doves. Before

we crossed oceans, she packed
    each one with great care, shielding

each page from the years. I was
        five—too young to care about

the past. But now, as her hair silvers
        under the light bulb, the years pass

the girl who once complained
        about Xi'an rain—the girl who released

five stamped doves into the sky.
        They even pass the five doves

now, hiding in the last drawer
        of the last bookshelf we search.

Unfolding each page, she tries
        to keep pace with the train

she rode while writing them, zipping
        Mongolia shut on her way to Xi'an. Now

she swallows smoke from the stove
        that keeps her anchored as she reads, that

keeps shrouding her from sight.

**2nd**

## Interim
### *Lindsay Li*

*for my brother*

After you left, I found
words I could not say
for fear of melting them

down in my mouth like ice.
*Vanilla, poltergeist, paramour.*
Words whose beauty slipped

away beneath the dark lake
of a half-life—where beauty goes
once we no longer recognize it.

*Cacophony. Serendipity.* You
said I had a storybook
for a mind, but in the moment

where it mattered most, I could
only hack out a curse, as if
I'd swallowed tumbleweeds

instead of ink. *Incandescent.*
All my life, I sought beautiful
passages to watch flutter, like moths

across a bathroom mirror, buzzing
hollow-eyed at their own reflection.
When my vocabulary failed me

I'd search up synonyms for *beautiful*
and later the moments that could
almost quantify you. *Idyllic, petrichor*.

It was raining when you left, as if
this were all a show on a channel
I was too dazed to switch off. I stayed

## Category 25: Russ and Ellen Notar World Vision Poetry Award

Celebrating the world and its many languages and people or commenting upon the world in which we live. 48-line limit.

1st Prize: "Nocturne for the Fort Greene Girls" by Adelaide Sendlenski
2nd Prize: "Summertime Epiphany" by Lindsay Li

3rd Prize: "Eldest Daughter" by Genevieve Watson
HM: "Learning Welsh" by Elizabeth Spragins


**Judge:** Nicole Yurcaba
**Sponsor:** Susan Notar

**1st**

## Nocturne for the Fort Greene Girls
### *Adelaide Sendlenski*

dusk is streaming onto the sidewalk
snaking through fort greene park. we repave

the pavement with Drake, with Kendrick
& Future. we stash our dreams of college

and driving lessons in the worn pockets
of our hoodies, stained with eyebrow pencils the color

of wilting  rose petals. we cake
mascara, charred as charcoal, on our lashes to hide

the false rumors swelling on our lids, the broken
families we keep locked in our pupils. instead, we smother

blue-razz gloss across our lips, parting them
only for first kisses and for breath to carry the stories

& dreams we  share on benches near rain soaked tennis courts.
we dab concealer, still moist-in-the-middle, still

two-shades-too-light or two-shades-too-dark, on our cheeks
covering yesterday's blemishes like secret confessions, so we may

grow into tomorrow's beauty and unfettered strength
with our arms linked—we are the girls of fort greene

& we hold the American Dream on bated breath.

**2nd**

## Summertime Epiphany at the
## Long Men Bay Hotspot

*Lindsay Li*


It's summer & I don't want anything
but milk tea and hotpot, even though


it's overpriced at $80. I stopped writing.
I've written two stories about men dying


over nothing at all. Funny, students like me feel less
suicidal in summer, even if the CDC says


otherwise. I've experienced a kind of death,
sleeping through the cricket-spun evenings. In July, nostalgia


pollinates my backyard as melancholy beats its wings
in my throat. At sixteen, I'm slogging through


my mid-life crisis' mid-life crisis: I am tired. But
what right do I have to be? In sixteen years


my grandmother will succumb to amnesia, and someday
to a creaking stop. That is when I will cry


properly. I would've been a good grandchild if only I hadn't
noticed myself withering from girl to nothing

**Li,** Summertime Epiphany at the Long Men Bay Hotspot, cont'd.


but *tanghulu* skewers for bones. I miss heatstroke
and mango ice cream bars in the Forbidden City, trips

to the corner store in building #4 for groceries, stopping
for a fresh slice of carrot cake and orange juice

at the so-called Jamaican café, no concentrate. Perhaps
the mirages have gotten me. Pile the fried rice on

before I forget to eat, yeah?

## Category 26: Spoken Word & Verse Video Contest

A video of a poet/poets (not more than 4 poets) reading/reciting an original poem 2-4 minutes in length.

1st Prize: "Marvel" by Stephanie Lask
2nd Prize: "The Hidden Body Beneath Sand Dunes" by Fairouz Bsharat

3rd Prize: "The More the Merrier" by Adele Gardner
HM: "Mission" by Derek Kannemeyer

**Judge:** Sharran C. Taylor aka Kween Yakini
**Sponsor:** Nathan Richardson

To watch the video, scan the QR code or
copy the link, and paste
the URL into your web browser's address bar.

**1st** **Marvel**
**Stephanie Lask**
YouTube Link: https://www.youtube.com/
watch?v=Reoc0jVN-mw

**2nd** **The Hidden Body Beneath Sand**
**Dunes**
**Fairouz Bsharat**

YouTube Link: https://youtu.be/3RxzS60QtSE

**3rd** **The More the Merrier**
**Adele Gardner**

YouTube Link: https://youtu.be/sm_2VD04WS0

**HM** **Mission**
**Derek Kannemeyer**

YouTube Link: https://www.youtube.com/watch?v=-
4YhgJ37Mt4

All of these videos are found on the YouTube channel:
Virginia Poetry Events@VirginiaPoets7859

https://www.youtube.com/playlist?list= PLKQdSGjC4F
UqQNg-GrZ4d1gO1FFRSDdqp

# Virginia Poetry 2025
## Biographies
## 1st and 2nd Place Poets

**Aaliyah Anderson** is a Black and Asian American student at the University of Mary Washington planning to study English (Creative Writing) and American Studies. Her work appears in *Beaver Mag, BarBar, coalitionworks*, and elsewhere. Winner of the Poetry Society of America's 2024 Student Award, Aaliyah is obsessed with burnt cheese and intersectional storytelling.

**Bill Ayres'** third book, *We Share the World*, will be published in 2025. It includes several PSV contests winning poems from the last few years (as well as poems published in *Commonweal, The Hollins Critic*, and others) His first 2 books are *What Passes for Wisdom* and *Jesus Poems*.

**Elizabeth Black** is an artist and poet living in Northern Virginia. She has published in the United States and abroad and has been honored with various awards for her poems and paintings. She was recently awarded first place in an international tanka sequence and nominated for a pushcart. She is delighted to be recognized by PSV in 2024 and 2025. Elizabeth finds inspiration for art and poetry in the natural world.

**Laura J. Bobrow** continues to find excitement in exploring the intricacies of the English language. More than 100 of her poems have appeared over the years in various media including a fourth-grade textbook in Abu Dhabi. She is also well-known as a professional storyteller.

**Fairouz Bsharat** is a Literary Arts major at Appomattox Regional Governor's School and the Virginia Youth Poet Laureate for Chester! She won first place in Fledge's National Nonfiction Competition and received a Scholastic Gold Medal and American Voices Award. To keep up with her work follow her @fairouzpoetry on Instagram.

**John Thornton Casey** has a Ph.D. from N.Y. University in teaching writing. He has published short stories in magazines such as Epoch; and has worked as a freelance editor for *Newsweek* and NASA. He has taught writing, literature, drama, film, and art appreciation from high school to higher education. He is married, has four daughters, and lives with his wife in Virginia. When not writing, he walks in the woods.

**Ann Chinnis** is the author of two poetry chapbooks-*Poppet, My Poppet* and *I Can Catch Anything*, forthcoming in April, as well as the recipient of a Pushcart Prize, 2025. Her work has been published in *Sky Island Journal, River Heron Review, Gyroscope, Crab Creek Review*, among others. She is an Emergency Physician from Virginia Beach.

**Jacqueline Davey** lives in Oakton, Virginia. She had a long career in publishing and marketing. She currently studies with George Mason University's MFA Creative Writing Program. She is a winner in the *Fairfax County Library's 2023* Poetry Contest. She has been published in *Persimmon Tree, Poetry Anthology: Star Gazing, Nap Lit Magazine*, and *Northern Virginia Bards Poetry Anthologies*.

**Maggie Dillow** grew up writing an embarrassing amount of terrible teen poetry in Chicagoland. She's the founding member of the Post-apocalyptic Poets for a Pre-apocalyptic World, a collective dedicated to performance-based poetics, and co-host of the podcast, *Girlhood Movie Database*. She has an MFA in Creative Writing from Hollins University and lives in Roanoke.

**S. Preston Duncan** is the author of *Blood Alluvium* (Parlyaree Press), *The Sound in This Time of Being* (BIGWRK), and co- creator of *Lost Arcana*. His poetry has been commissioned by The Peace Studio, shortlisted for the Art of Creative Unity Award, nominated for Pushcart and Best of the Net, and appeared in dozens of journals including *Image, [PANK],* and *HAD*.

**Eric Forsbergh** has published over 100 poems in the US and UK, and two full length poetry books, the most recent being *This Mortal Coil, Poems of DNA*. He has twice won the Edgar Allen Poe Prize. A retired DDS, he has participated in two health mission trips in the jungles of Guatemala. He is a Vietnam veteran.

**Chapman Hood Frazier's** *The Lost Books of the Bestiary was* published in 2023 by V Press LC. His work has appeared in *The Virginia Quarterly Review, The Southern Poetry Review* and has won numerous awards. Currently a Professor Emeritus from James Madison University, he lives in Rice, Virginia and is co-managing Bellfield Farm LLC, a writer's retreat.

**Mark Fryburg** practiced journalism in Roanoke, then public relations and flight instruction in his native Oregon. Diving into poetry when he returned to the Roanoke Valley in 2022, this late- blooming septuagenarian received a First Place in PSV's contest and an Honorable Mention in *Passager Journal's* national competition last year.

**Adele Gardner** (they/them) is a fiction writer & award-winning poet with a poetry collection, _Halloween Hearts_, (Jackanapes Press) who has written 500 stories, poems, art, and articlesin *Analog Science Fiction and Fact, Clarkesworld, Strange Horizons, PodCastle, Daily Science Fiction*, and others. They are a member of the Poetry Society of Virginia. This genderfluid, pan night owl loves libraries, samurai films, and reading comics with cats. Adele serves as literary executor for father, mentor, and namesake Delbert R. Gardner and is co-chair of the 2022 Dwarf Stars Award with Greer Woodward: https://sfpoetry.com/ ds/22dwarfstars.html

**Mark G. Hammerschick** writes poetry and fiction. He holds a BA in English from the University of Illinois at Champaign-Urbana and a BS and MBA. He began writing in grade school and has contributed several poems to literary journals over the years and has been published sporadically.

**Jane Harkness** is a freelance writer and poet. Her work has received awards from the Hampton Roads Writers Conference and the Christopher Newport University Writers Conference. Born and raised in Beach Haven, NJ, she now lives in Norfolk, VA

**Mark Hudson** has several pieces accepted for the "Making the Unseen Seen" ekphrastic anthology, which will be published in summer, 2025 (High Tide Publications, Deltaville, Virginia). The irony? Growing up, science was one of Mark Hudson's worst topics! Mark Hudson likes to learn new things through writing poetry. He likes to spend time at the library!

**Lorraine Jeffery** has won numerous prizes and published over 200 poems in journals including *Westward Quarterly, Ibbetson St., Clockhouse, Orchard Press, Naugatuck River Review, Halcyone* and *Tahoma*. Her first book, *When the Universe Brings Us Back* was published in 2022. Her chapbook, *Tethers*, was published by Kelsay Books in 2023 and they also published *Saltwater Soul* in 2024.

**Derek Kannemeyer's** recent poetry books include *Scattershots* and *Found Voices* (2025), *You Go In By the Gate That Isn't There* (2023), *A Betabestiary* (2022), and *Mutt Spirituals* (2021). His novel *The Memory Addicts* appeared in 2022. Kirkus Reviews listed his photography/ nonfiction work *Unsay Their Names* as one of their 100 Best Indie Books of 2022. His website is www. petalridge.com.

**Steven Knepper** is Bruce C. Gottwald, Jr. '81 Chair for Academic Excellence at Virginia Military Institute and the editor of *New Verse Review: A Journal of Lyric and Narrative Poetry*. His poems have been published in many journals, including fine Virginia publications such as *Roanoke Review, Rappahannock Review, William and Mary Review*, and *Floyd County Moonshine*."

**Stephanie Lask aka Steph Love** is a spoken word artist, teaching artist, event host, web designer and graphic designer originally from Virginia Beach, VA. She is also the slam master for the nationally ranked Verb Benders Slam Team and serves on the Board of Directors for Southern Fried Poetry Slam, Inc. Stephanie is a hip hop junkie, vinyl collector and cat lady currently residing in Norfolk, VA.

**Rebecca K. Leet** has spent a lifetime across the Potomac River from Washington, DC, seeing the best of times and the worst. Writing poetry keeps her sane. She has been published online, in journals and anthologies, and on buses. Her book *Living With the Doors Wide Open* was published in 2018.

**Lindsay Li** is a Chinese American writer based in the Bay Area. In her free time, she attempts to unite history with the coming future, goes down Wikipedia rabbit holes, and writes anything that comes to mind.

**Kindra McDonald** is the author of the collections *Teaching a Wild Thing, Fossils* and *In the Meat Years*. She received her MFA from Queens University of Charlotte and is a poet artist working and teaching in mixed-media and found poetry. You can find her in the woods or at www.kindramcdonald.com

**Mac Mestayer** is an experimental physicist who recently retired from Jefferson Lab, a national accelerator center for nuclear physics. His research focused on the quark structure of protons and neutrons. His hobbies include hiking, bird- watching, wood sculpture and poetry. He lives In Williamsburg, Va. with his wife Kathi.

**The Reverend Joel Stephen Neubauer** lives in Virginia with spouse Danielle and child Galilee Grace. Joel first explored poetry with educators valuing humanities and communication arts: Montgomery County (Maryland) Public Schools; William & Mary (BS '03); United Lutheran Seminary (MDiv '07, STM '19). Still adoring poetries of "the Word made flesh," Joel is pastor of St Mark Lutheran Church, Yorktown.

**Richard Eric Pound ("Eric")** was born in 1950 in Indiana. A retired CIA operations officer and senior executive, he lives now in Williamsburg with his wife Sharon, a talented artist. The past year has been eventful, with the publication of Eric's first book, *I Went Aviatin' to China*, and his first entry into the Annual PSV Contests.

**Lynne Schmidt** is the queer, neurodivergent grandchild of a Holocaust survivor, and a therapist with a focus in trauma and healing. They are the 2025 Maine Arts Fellow for Literary Arts and the author of *Dying Dog Poems*, *The Unaccounted for Circles of Hell*, *SexyTime*, which was a winner of the 2021 The Poetry Question Chapbook Contest, *Dead Dog Poems* which was the 2020 New Women's Voices Contest, and *Gravity*, which has been listed as One of the Best Breakup Books of All Time by Book Authority. When given the choice, Lynne prefers their pack of dogs and one cat to humans.

**Adelaide Sendlenski** is a student at Saint Ann's School in Brooklyn. She was born in New York and raised in Sydney, Australia. An avid classicist and language enthusiast, Adelaide devotes her spare time to reading Latin, Ancient Greek and Sanskrit. Her poetry has been featured in *The Slowdown* and has been internationally recognized by the Scholastic Art & Writing Awards, Hollins University, Woorilla, the Brooklyn Public Library, the New York Society Library, Poetry Society of Virginia and more. Her up-and-coming literary magazine, *The Antigone Project*, empowers a range of young adult voices in the Classics.

**Allen Weber** lives in Hampton, Virginia with his poet wife and two of their three sons. His poems have appeared in numerous journals and anthologies—including *Arc Poetry Magazine, The Fourth River, Iris Literary Journal, Naugatuck River Review, Splash*—Haunted Waters Press, *Terrain, Unlikely Stories*, and *Up the Staircase Quarterly*.

**Erin Newton Wells** is a teacher, artist, and writer currently living in Charlottesville, Virginia, where she is content to observe the world and write about it.

**Denise Wilcox** is an award-winning author who writes poetry and nonfiction for all ages. Her work has been published in the 2023 American Book Award Best Poetry Anthology, *Dear Human at the Edge of Time*, as well as *Paterson Literary Review, Quilted Poems, Blended Poems, Views of Virginia, Gathering, Ladybug Magazine* and *FunforKidz*. Denise lives in Northern Virginia where she greets each day as a blessing and each encounter with nature, family, friends and ordinary life as inspiration.

**Diana Woodcock** has authored seven chapbooks and seven poetry collections, most recently *Reverent Flora ~ The Arabian Desert's Botanical Bounty* (Shanti Arts), *Heaven Underfoot* (2022 Codhill Press Pauline Uchmanowicz Poetry Award), *Holy Sparks* (2020 Paraclete Press Poetry Award finalist) and *Facing Aridity* (2020 Prism Prize for Climate Literature finalist). A three-time Pushcart Prize nominee and Best of the Net nominee, she currently teaches at VCUarts Qatar. https:// www.dianawoodcock.com/; https://qatar.vcu.edu/news/our- faculty/dr-diana-g-woodcock/

**Minnie Wu** is a junior at The Pennington School. Her poetry and prose have been published in *The Shore, San Pedro River Review, SWWIM Everyday, Blue Marble Review*, and more. She participated in the 2024 Adroit Journal Summer Mentorship Program and won the 2025 YoungArts award in poetry. Outside of writing, Minnie enjoys a cup of warm matcha latte and spending time with her pets.

# Virginia Poetry 2025
## Judge Biographies

**Patsy Asuncion's** Cut on the Bias & Lineage of Weeds plus feature in The Best 64 Poets of 2019 depict her world slant as a bi-racial, first-generation immigrant. Her third, A Universal Belonging, will be out in August by Kelsay Books. Patsy promotes diversity through: publications (e.g., New York Times and 20+ anthologies; presentations (workshops and judging); other activities (open mic with 25,200+ YouTube views and arts boards.

**Randy Brooks** is Professor of English Emeritus at Millikin University, where he teaches a haiku course. Randy and Shirley Brooks are publishers of Brooks Books and co-editors of *Mayfly* haiku magazine. His most recent books include *Walking the Fence: Selected Tanka* and *The Art of Reading and Writing Haiku*. His website is: http:// www.brooksbookshaiku.com/

**Laura Bylenok** is the author of *Living Room* (University of Nebraska Press), winner of the Backwaters Prize in Poetry; *Warp* (Truman State University Press), winner of the T.S. Eliot Prize; and *a/0* (New Michigan Press). She is an Associate Professor of English at the University of Mary Washington in Fredericksburg, Virginia.

**Angela M. Carter** is a poet, novelist, speaker, artist, and advocate. A 2014 Pushcart Prize nominee, she authored *Memory Chose a Woman's Body* and the upcoming *Love is the Dying Dog* (2nd Avenue Press, 06/2025). Her work,featured in acclaimed journals, blends raw vulnerability with resilience, inspiring truth, healing, and empowerment through poetry, storytelling, and advocacy.

**Terry Cox-Joseph** is former president of The Poetry Society of Virginia and a former newspaper reporter. Her poetry chapbook, *Between Then and Now,* was published by Finishing Line Press. She was coordinator for the annual Christopher Newport University Writers' Conference and Contest for ten years. An award-winning poet, she has been published internationally.

**Dr. Kathleen P. Decker** was Vice President of the Poetry Society of Virginia from 2019-2025. Poetry books include *Russian Reverie, Whispers on Paper, Essence of Woman* (Laughing CyPress), *Updraft*, and *Fishmas* (High Tide Publications). She edited anthologies including: *MyNeighbor's Life* and *On Crimson Wings*, (Laughing CyPress) and *Quilted Poems, Views of Virginia*, (Poetry Society of Virginia), and *Blended Voices* (High Tide Publications).

**Joanne Durham** is the author of *To Drink from a Wider Bowl*, winner of the Sinclair Poetry Prize (Evening Street Press 2022) and the chapbook, *On Shifting Shoals* (Kelsay 2023). She won the 2025 Miriam Chaikin Poetry Prize. Her poems appear in many journals and anthologies, including *Poetry South, Poetry East, CALYX, and NC Literary Review*. She lives on the North Carolina coast, with the ocean as her backyard and muse. https://www. joannedurham.com

**Stan Galloway** teaches at Bridgewater College and spends his nights in a cabin in the hills of West Virginia. He has authored/(co-)edited 11 books, most recently, *Savor: Poems for the Tongue* (Friendly City Books, 2024).

**Claudia Gary** teaches workshops on Sonnet, Villanelle, Meter, Poetry vs. Trauma at The Writer's Center (writer.org) and privately, currently via Zoom. Author of *Humor Me* (2006) and chapbooks including *Genetic Revisionism* (2019), she is an advisory editor of *New Verse Review*. Her 2022 article on setting poems to music is online at https://straightlabyrinth.info/conference.html.

**Bill Glose** undertakes intriguing pursuits to write about such as walking across Virginia and participating in a world-record- setting skinny dip. The author of five poetry collections and hundreds of magazine articles, Bill Glose was featured by NPR on The Writer's Almanac in 2017 and won the Library of Virginia Award for Fiction in 2023 for his book *All the Ruined Men*.

**Kim Hazelwood** is the founder and poetry editor of *The Green Silk Journal*, online since 2005. *Modern European Poetry*, 1970, edited by Willis Barnstone, greatly inspired her early days, providing much passion and variety for the creative zing great poetry provides. Influences also include: T.S. Eliot, Walt Whitman, Wallace Stevens, many others. *Jungle Light*, a new poetry collection is coming soon.

**Henry Hart** teaches English at the College of William and Mary. He has published four books of poetry, the most recent being *Familiar Ghosts*. He has also published several books about modern poets, including *Seamus Heaney's Gifts* (LSU, 2024) which won the Lewis P. Simpson Award.

**Dr. Patricia Hopkins** is an Assistant professor of English and Director of African-American Studies at Christopher Newport University, where she researches violence inflicted upon the black female body and images of black motherhood in literature. She is a recipient of a Woodrow Wilson National Fellowship Foundation, Career Enhancement Fellowship for Junior Faculty.

**John Hoppenthaler's** books of poetry are *Night Wing Over Metropolitan Area, Domestic Garden, Anticipate the Coming Reservoir,* and *Lives of Water*, all with Carnegie Mellon UP. Professor of English at East Carolina University, his poetry appears in *Ploughshares, Virginia Quarterly Review, TriQuarterly, Southern Review, Poetry Northwest, McSweeney's Internet Tendency, Blackbird, Southern Humanities Review*, and many other journals and anthologies.

**Luisa A. Igloria** is the author of *Caulbearer* (Immigrant Writing Series Prize, Black Lawrence Press, 2024), *Maps for Migrants and Ghosts* (Co-Winner, 2019 Crab Orchard Open Poetry Prize), 13 other books, and 4 chapbooks. She is the Louis I. Jaffe and University Professor of English and Creative Writing at Old Dominion University's MFA Creative Writing Program and leads workshops for and is a member of the Board of The Muse Writers Center in Norfolk. Luisa is a Virginia Poet Laureate Emerita (2020-22). The Academy of American Poets awarded her a 2021 Poet Laureate Fellowship. www.luisaigloria.com

**Kirk Judd**, a lifelong West Virginian, was a member of the Appalachian Literary League, a founding member of West Virginia Writers, and a founding member of Allegheny Echoes. The author of 3 collections of poetry and a co-editor of the widely acclaimed anthology, "Wild, Sweet Notes – 50 Years of West Virginia Poetry 1950 – 1999", he is widely published.

**Joanna Lee** is a doctor, poet, and small business owner, and is a founder of writing community River City Poets and the current Poet Laureate for the city of Richmond. A four- time alum of Tupelo Press' 30/30 Project, she is the author of the chapbook *Dissections* and co-editor of the anthology *Lingering in the Margins*.

**Catherine McCormack** is a retired freelance writer living in Virginia. During her 30 year career, she freelanced in a variety of fields including speeches, book reviews, historical articles, grant proposals and fiction. But poetry was always in the background. Often published in literary journals, she also found unique homes for poems, like the USMC magazine, Leatherneck. She judged poetry and fiction contests. She was bestowed an Honorary Lifetime Membership for her PSV work through the 1980's and 90's.

**Nathaniel Perry** is the author of two books of poetry, Nine Acres (Copper Canyon, 2011) and Long Rules (Backwaters, 2021), and a book of essays, Joy (Or Something Darker but Like It) (Univ. Of Michigan, 2024). He teaches at Hampden- Sydney College.

**Nathan M. Richardson** is a published author, performance poet and Frederick Douglass Historian. He is the author of four collections of poetry and teaches a variety of workshops for emerging writers and spoken word artists. Nathan is now in the 11th year of The Frederick Douglass Speaking Tour - a living history performance that captures completely the physical, spiritual and intellectual essence of the former slave, writer, orator and abolitionist Frederick Douglass. Learn more about Nathan's work at www. scpublishing.com poetry that blends American history and storytelling. Because of Kween's literary works she has been able to perform for audiences throughout Hampton Roads.

**David Anthony Sam** lives in Virginia with his wife, Linda. His poetry has appeared in over 100 journals. Eight of his poetry collections are in print including Writing the Significant Soil (2023, winner of the Homebound Poetry Prize). A ninth, Geographies of the Dead, was published in 2025.

**Lisa Russ Spaar** is the author of fourteen books, most recently *Madrigalia: New & Selected Poems* (Persea Books, 2021) and a novel, *Paradise Close* (Persea Books, 2022). A new collection of poems, *Soul Cake*, will appear in 2026. Her honors include a Rona Jaffe Award, Guggenheim Fellowship, Library of Virginia Prize for Poetry, and Carol Weinstein Prize. She is Professor of English at the University of Virginia.

**Sharran C. Taylor** also known as **Kween Yakini**, is a five times published poetry book author, a Spoken Word Artist, a multi recipient of the Nat Turner Library Black Literature Awards, a Black American History community presenter. Kween Yakini has a distinct style of writing.

**Frederick Wilbur's** poetry collections are *As Pus Floats the Splinter Out*, *Conjugation of* Perhaps and *The Heft of Promise*. His work appears in many periodicals including *Atlanta Review, Hampden-Sydney Poetry Review, Midwest Quarterly* (Stephen Meats Poetry Prize, 2018), *One Art: a journal of poetry, Shenandoah, South Carolina Review, and Southern Poetry Review*. He is poetry co-editor for *Streetlight Magazine*.

**Nicole Yurcaba** (Нікола Юрцаба) is a Ukrainian American of Hutsul/ Lemko origin. Her poems and reviews have appeared in *Appalachian Heritage, Atlanta Review, Seneca Review, New Eastern Europe,* and Ukraine's *Euromaidan Press, Lit Gazeta, Chytomo, Bukvoid,* and *The New Voice of Ukraine*.

**Kristin Camitta Zimet** is the author of Take in My Arms the Dark, a collection of poetry, and the co-author of A Tender Time: Quaker Voices on the End of Life. She was a co-founder of the Appalachian Center for Poets and Writers and the editor of The Sow's Ear Poetry Review. Her poetry has been published in journals and anthologies in eight countries; hung in museums, libraries, and art galleries; and performed in venues from concert hall to arboretum.

# Acknowledgments:

The Poetry Society of Virginia is deeply grateful to the individual sponsors of each category and to the judges who put hours of thought into choosing poems which represent excellent poetry. We would also like to recognize those who volunteer their time to put together the contest, this book, and to celebrate the winners of the 2025 Contests. This book could not be created without the support and creative genius of our publisher, Jeanne Johansen of High Tide Publications, Inc!

## The 2025 Contest Team

**Contest Chair:** Dr. Kathleen P. Decker

**Contest Book Editors:** Dr. Kathleen P. Decker

Aderonke Adeleke, Assistant Editor

**Contest Award Ceremony Emcee:** Nan Ottenritter

**Award Certificates:** Gail Giewont

**Prizes:** Issued by PSV Treasurer W. David Hubbard

**Thank you all for an amazing team!**

# Index
# 1st and 2nd Place Poems
# By Poet

# Index

## J

Lorraine Jeffery  68

## K

Derek Kannemeyer  15, 34, 99
Steven Knepper  14, 18, 22

## L

Stephanie Lask  116
Rebecca Leet  43
Lindsay Li  48, 76, 81, 108, 113

## M

Mac Mestayer 31
Kindra McDonald  77

## N

Joel Stephen Neubauer  72

## P

Richard Eric Pound  50

## S

Lynne Schmidt  54
Adelaide Sendlenski  80, 90, 112

## W

Allen Weber  35
Erin Newton Wells  60, 95
Denise Wilcox  40
Diana Woodcock  64
Minnie Wu  106

www.ingramcontent.com/pod-product-compliance
Lightning Source LLC
Chambersburg PA
CBHW072030170626
46811CB00008B/3013